Successful Solutions to Buying Your Home

Realizing

How To Buy A House Using A VA Loan

How to Buy a Home Using a VA Loan

What Every Home Buyer Should Know

Author

Stacey Chillemi

Successful Solutions to Buying Your Home: Realizing

How to Buy a Home Using a VA Loan

What Every Home Buyer Should Know

By Stacey Chillemi

LULU EDITION

PUBLISHED BY:

Stacey Chillemi on Lulu

How to Buy a Home Using a VA Loan

ISBN: 978-1-105-52392-2

How to Buy a Home

Using a VA Loan

Successful Solutions to Buying Your Home

MASTERING THE ART OF

Successful Real Estate Buying

How VA Loans Can Get You the Home of Your Dreams

Succeed in Accomplishing Your Dreams

Life comes with obstacles,

Obstacles that must be pursued,

No matter how rough the obstacle,

No matter how long and how tough the walk

You will succeed by trying your best,

Failure does not exist if you try,

*Taking "**one day at a time**,*

You cannot change the past,

The best is yet to come,

The present is now,

Focus and work on the present,

Success will follow in the future,

Focus on the goals that you create for yourself,

Change is wonderful,

Do not fear change,

Change is wonderful,

Today is the beginning to a new destiny,

The mind is a powerful tool that has the strength to achieve,

Create a plan to help you achieve what destiny has in store for you

Preparation is the key to help you succeed in buying your new home

Table of Contents

PREFACE

The purpose of the VA loan is to offer our service men and women the opportunity of home ownership; a reward for having served faithfully. If you served in the military you could qualify for a VA Home Loan, if you are a U.S. military veteran, or if you are currently serving our country and have been on active duty for a minimum of 90 days. A VA Home Loan provides special benefits. It is usually the best choice of financing available to eligible borrowers. In this eBook, you will learn why choosing a VA Home Loan is such a great option for homebuyers. We will also summarize the home buying process to demonstrate how easy it is to become a homeowner just by utilizing your VA eligibility.

Section 1 – Preparing to buy a home: a little planning can make all the difference

INTRODUCTION

Almost everybody has a dream home. A place they like to stroll through in their thoughts, choosing make-believe paint colors for the walls and putting pretend curtains up. However, too many people's dream homes remain just that–dreams, but it doesn't have to be like that at all. The dreams of owning a home has become a reality for millions of Americans by using VA loans to help purchase their home.

Our eBook, ***"How to Buy a Home Using a VA Loan,"*** contains valuable educational information, tips, techniques and guidelines for buying a home using a VA Loan.

This eBook describes the tools and techniques that will teach you how to prepare, qualify and purchase your home successfully using a VA Loan. This eBook includes plenty of examples, guidelines and instructions to make buying your home with a VA Loan a smooth, easy and quick process.

1. WHAT IS A VA LOAN?

Knowing Is the Key to Successful Home Purchase

IF YOU DREAM IT, YOU CAN DO IT!

BUYING A HOME WITH A VA LOAN

A Dream Is Just a Dream
A Goal
Is a Dream with a Plan to Accomplish and Achieve That Dream

Did you know…?

The VA has guaranteed over 18 million home loans since 1944 when it set out to help Veterans achieve their goals of home ownership.

The Realty World
Helping Someone's Dream Become
"A Dream Come True"

The VA Loan became known in 1944 through the original Servicemen's Readjustment Act also known as the GI Bill of Rights. President Franklin D. Roosevelt signed the GI Bill into law. The bill provided veterans with a federally guaranteed home with no down payment. This was designed to provide housing and assistance for veterans and their families, and the dream of home ownership became a reality for millions of veterans. The GI Bill contributed more than any other program in history to the welfare of veterans and their families, and to the growth of the nation's economy.

With more than 25.5 million veterans and service personnel eligible for VA financing, this loan is attractive and has many advantages. Eligibility for the VA loan is defined as Veterans who served on active duty and have a discharge other than dishonorable after a minimum of 90 days of service during wartime or a minimum of 181 continuous days during peacetime. There is a two-year requirement if the veteran enlisted and began service after September 7, 1980 or was an officer and began service after October 16, 1981. There is a six-year requirement for National guards and reservists with certain criteria and there are specific rules concerning the eligibility of surviving spouses.

VA will guarantee a maximum of 25 percent of a home loan amount up to $104,250, which limits the maximum loan amount to $417,000. Generally, the reasonable value of the property or the purchase price, whichever is less, plus the funding fee may be borrowed. All veterans must qualify, for they are not automatically eligible for the program.

VA guaranteed loans are made by private lenders, such as banks, savings & loans, or mortgage companies to eligible veterans for the purchase of a home, which must be for their own personal occupancy. The guaranty means the lender is protected against loss if you or a later owner fails to repay the loan. The guaranty replaces the protection the lender normally receives by requiring a down payment allowing you to obtain favorable financing terms.

Reasons to Get A VA Loan:

- ✓ You do not have to have a down payment.

- ✓ Other homebuyers may have to save for years to afford their first home, with a VA loan, you can be ready immediately.

- ✓ VA Loans generally have lower interest rates than most conventional loans, which mean more affordable monthly payments.

- ✓ Veterans who get a VA Loan do not have to pay what is known in the conventional loan world as PMI, or private mortgage insurance. This is another factor that lowers the monthly mortgage payment on VA Loans.

- ✓ With recent changes in the mortgage market, it is considerably easier to qualify for a VA Loan than a conventional loan.

- ✓ 80% of those who qualify for VA Loans could not have qualified for a conventional mortgage because with the Veterans Administration backing these loans, a mortgage company is able to take a risk on a loan that they would not normally take.

2. PREPARATION

Preparation Is the Key to Successful Home Purchase

IF YOU DREAM IT, YOU CAN DO IT!

BUYING A HOME WITH A VA LOAN

A Dream Is Just a Dream
A Goal
Is a Dream with a Plan to Accomplish and Achieve That Dream

The Realty World

Helping Someone's Dream Become "A Dream Come True"

Did you know…?

The VA guaranteed 314,000 VA loans in

Buying a home is one of the most important decisions you will ever make in your entire life and it should be a fun and joyful experience as well. Purchasing a home does not have to be stressful. It should be positive experience that will set the stage with new beginnings to explore.

In order to make purchasing a home a successful and memorable one you need to prepare and create a productive plan including long and short-term goals. Buying a home mainly depends on how well prepared you are during the process. A lot of research and thought goes into selecting your home and then purchasing it using a VA loan at a suitable price.

Here are a few guidelines to consider before buying a home…

- **Why do you want to purchase a home? -** The first question you need to ask yourself is why are you buying a home? Do not simply use reasons like *'Everyone needs a home', 'It is an investment'* and so forth. It is not that these are bad reasons for owning a home but they should be valid to you as a person or family. A house is primarily a place you can live in. Having your own home does have a number of advantages like tax benefits, investment source, and so on. But it does give the owner a feeling of pride and sense of achievement. However, all these are just secondary benefits. By knowing exactly why you are buying a house, you will be able to focus clearly on the task and are unlikely to be abstracted.

- ✓ **Begin creating a budget -** Although buying a home has a tendency to become an emotional affair, you should never lose track of the financial aspect involved. Before you take the plunge, it is advisable to spend some time taking stock of your assets and available finances. Even before you start going out to look at homes, you should decide on an upper price limit. This is the most you are willing to pay for the house. Your current budget should be the main factor in deciding the price limit. Do not be swayed by your real estate agent into buying something overpriced. The agent's commission depends on the price of the house, and it is natural that he would want a larger amount as his commission. You alone are the best judge of deciding how much you are willing to pay. Another reason why budget is important is to have a house that you can afford to buy and still live comfortably while paying your house loan. Just because you have bought, a house does not mean other expenditures no longer matter. You will still need money every month to be able to buy food, pay the bills, school fees, other loan payments, etc. You should strike a balance between paying for your house and making all your other payments. You may have to cut back on certain non-essential expenditures like fancy dinners, expensive gadgets, and so on to meet budgetary constraints.

- ✓ **Research and learn as much as you can about the VA loan process** - Nowadays, it is virtually impossible to buy a house outright. This is why many military families purchase their home using a VA loan. It is very important for you to understand how the VA loan process works. You need to understand what it consists of, how to qualify, how to buy, and how to close. There are many things to consider, so don't leave it up to the realtors friends and your family to inform you about everything it involves. Do your homework, so you can ask questions, be well informed and this will help you avoid any unwanted surprises. Take responsibility and do the best you can to learn about the entire process. Remember that all financial institutions have their own rules and regulations. Also, check what documents are to be submitted when you apply for your VA loan.

Helpful Tip: Talk to people who have recently purchased homes through VA to get an idea of how the process works.

Did you know…?

The government is loaning 100% of the cost of the home to you, even the financing is included.

There Is No Better Time to Start Planning Than the Present

Ever hear the saying, ***"no better time than the present,"*** and this is especially true when you are contemplating about purchasing a home and preparing for the application process. There is a lot that a VA loan underwriter needs to consider before approving a loan to you as a potential homebuyer. Preparing this important documentation in advance can save you valuable time in the underwriting process and can get you a home of your own a lot quicker.

Before you apply for the VA Loan, the first thing you should do is gather all the necessary paperwork as possible. This will help shorten the entire loan process, so you can obtain your VA Loan a lot faster. During the loan process there may be other things you are asked to acquire, but if you gather all the required information before hand you will probably be able to get the ball rolling and this will make the loan process a lot less stressful too.

What Can You Do To Prepare For The VA Loan Application Process?

There are three types of information you need to submit to an underwriter. **Those three things are:**

1. **Your personal information** - Your personal information is important to verify identification and

living arrangements. Your personal credit history will be analyzed as well using your Social Security number. *You will also need to provide:*

- ✓ **Current Address:** You will need to provide your residence address for the last two years.
- ✓ **Driver's License:** Should be a current driver's license or an official state identification.
- ✓ **Social Security Number:** Have your Social Security card available for authentication.
- ✓ **Green Card or Work Permit:** If you are living and working in the United States but are a citizen of another country, it is important to show verification of legal work status.

- ✓ **Certificate of Eligibility and DD-214:** (for Veterans only)

2. **Employment Information** - Your employment history and income is an important factor in determining whether you can afford a mortgage and have steady employment to continue to pay a monthly mortgage.

   - ✓ **Current Pay Stubs:** You should provide copies of the last two months of your employment pay stubs from all employers, verifying your current monthly income.

   - ✓ **Tax Returns and W-2's:** Your past two years of tax returns, along with your employer W-2 forms, should be submitted.

- ✓ **Name/Location of Employer(s):** Gather information from your employers for the past two years.

- ✓ **Self-Employed:** Self-employed individuals will need to provide at least three years of prior tax returns, as well as balance sheets and income/loss statements for the same time period.

- ✓ **Divorce and Spousal Support:** Individuals who are divorced and are receiving spousal support may include this information as part of their income.

3. **Savings Information** - Not only is your monthly income used to consider your financial mortgage obligation, but your savings and investments are an important asset to analyze what you are eligible for to pay as a down payment on your new home. These also demonstrate your financial reserves that

will keep you from failing to pay on your mortgage should you encounter employment difficulty, such as becoming layoff.

Below is the savings information that you will need to provide…

- ✓ **Bank Account Information:** You should provide copies of statements for the past three months of all bank accounts, including checking, savings, money market, certificates of deposit, etc.

- ✓ **Investment Accounts:** Recent statements of any investment accounts, including 401(k), mutual funds, stock market accounts, etc.

- ✓ **Other Real Estate:** Complete information should be provided on any other real estate assets that you own.

- ✓ **Personal Property:** A personal statement of the value of your personal property including furniture, jewelry, automobiles, and so forth.

VA loans are a good option for any current or previous homeowner to purchase a new home. The application process is extensive and the documentation noted above is essential for getting approval from a VA underwriter. But you can have an advantage before contacting a VA approved Loan Company. With some preparation, planning and research, you can get organized before making the application and be on your way to home ownership quicker than you anticipate.

After you have submitted your application, your loan goes through an automatic underwriting system, which gives approval for qualified applicants to go ahead to process the loan.

3. QUALIFY

Learn How to Qualify For A VA Loan

IF YOU DREAM IT, YOU CAN DO IT!

BUYING A HOME WITH A VA LOAN

A Dream Is Just a Dream
A Goal
Is a Dream with a Plan to Accomplish and Achieve That Dream

The Realty World
Helping Someone's Dream Become
"A Dream Come True"

As a Veteran, the first step in obtaining a VA Loan is to determine whether or not you are qualified to receive a VA loan. This determination is made based upon the type of service (active duty or reserve) and the timeframe.

Who Qualifies For A VA Loan?

Veterans who served active duty in the Armed Forces after World War II and were discharged under terms other than dishonorable are eligible for VA home loan benefits. During wartime periods, and active duty service, the veteran must have, at the minimum, 90 days of service on their records. If a veteran has served only during peacetime periods, the active service requirement is 180 days. This is true for active duty military personnel, as well. Enlisted service veterans who served after 1980 and officers who served after 1981 must have completed 2 years of service to be eligible. Selected Reserve and National Guard members are also eligible if they have served 6 years of service and were honorably discharged.

Some individuals, who do not meet the requirements for active or reserve duty, may still qualify.

These include the following:

- ✓ Spouses of deceased veterans, who died as a result of their active service, or a service related injury, are eligible if they have not remarried.
- ✓ Spouses of missing in action or prisoners of war are eligible for VA Loans as long as the service enlistee has been missing for over 90 days.
- ✓ U.S. citizens who served with an allied country during WWII may be eligible.

What Are The VA Loan Approval Requirements?

There are several requirements that must be met before your VA loan is approved...

1. **You must hold a valid Certificate of Eligibility:** You will need to prove you are qualified to receive the VA loan. As a veteran, you may obtain your COE by completing VA Form 26-1880, and mailing it, along with proof of military service, to an eligibility center. In many cases, it may be possible to obtain your COE from your lender using the ACE (automated certificate of eligibility) system.

2. **Your FICO score must be above 620 (a score above 640 is preferred):** As a sign of the times, mortgage investors across the country have made it a requirement that a borrower have a 620 FICO score or higher to qualify for a VA loan.

3. **You must take the loan for a valid purpose:** To be approved you must have a valid reason why you need this VA loan such as a house, townhouse, condominium or other governmentally approved reason.

4. **You must have a DD214:** You will need to submit a copy of your DD Form 214 release paper or Statement of Service if active military

5. **You must intend to occupy the house within a reasonable time after closing:** with your real estate agent's assistance, you may choose to sign a purchase contract conditioned on the approval of your VA home loan. A pre-approval from a VA lender will make this process easier, but does not necessarily replace the condition of final approval.

6. **Provide the lender with your COE and complete the loan application:** The lender will compile all credit and income information. They will also arrange for the VA licensed appraiser to determine the reasonable value for the property.

7. **Your credit must be satisfactory**

8. **Income:** The income you and your spouse receive must be established and adequate to pay the monthly mortgage.

9. **You must have the last 2 yrs. of your tax returns:** You will need to submit A copy of your W2's for the past 2 years or complete tax returns if self employed

10. **You must have copies of your past bank statements:** (preferably 2 months worth)

11. **You must have copies of your most recent pay stubs:** You will need to submit your last 30 days worth of pay stubs, showing your current year-to-date gross income.

12. **Submit Any Award Letters:** Present any award letters showing any disability, pension, or Social Security monies you are receiving

13. **Declarations Page:** You will to show a copy of the Declarations page from your Home Owner's Insurance policy

14. **Note:** You will need to submit a **"Note"** from your current mortgage company if you have one.

What Are The Benefits Of A VA Loan?

- ✓ No down payment (unless required by the lender)
- ✓ VA mortgage loans often offer lower interest rates than conventional loans
- ✓ Veteran Loans do not have mortgage insurance premiums
- ✓ Closing costs are comparable and may be lower than other loans
- ✓ Assumable mortgage
- ✓ VA home loan program is reusable for purchases and refinances

- ✓ No penalty for pre-payment
- ✓ You may qualify for a VA Loan when you cannot qualify for other mortgage loans
- ✓ VA assistance for veterans in default because of temporary financial difficulty

4. DO THE RESEARCH

Learn Why It Is Important To **Research** What You Want Before You Buy It

IF YOU DREAM IT, YOU CAN DO IT!

BUYING A HOME WITH A VA LOAN

A Dream Is Just a Dream
A Goal
Is a Dream with a Plan to Accomplish and Achieve That Dream

The Realty World
Helping Someone's Dream Become
"A Dream Come True"

"Be careful what you picture and write down because you'll get it," Skip Ross, National Public Speaker and Businessman

Priorities and Trade-Offs

What is most important to you about a home?

Buying a home is an exciting time for everyone. It is exciting for the family, for their close friends, and for the realtors. Yes, even the realtors. The realtors build the bridge, helping you cross over to new journey and page in your life.

One of the things you want to avoid when you buy a home is jumping right into buying the first home you see. Many people are so excited about buying a home that they buy one of the first few homes they see and afterwards they have some regret. For example, I should have bought a home with a basement or I should have got a colonial rather than a bi-level.

The best thing to do is to sit down with your other half and create a checklist by listing your wants and needs. The better you define what you want; the more likely that you will get it.

Example:

THINGS I NEED TO HAVE IN MY NEW HOME

THE MUST-HAVES

1. ***One wants an updated kitchen**
2. *** A two car-garage**
3. *** 3 bed/2bath**
4. ***The maximum price I can pay is under $260k.**
5.
6.
7.
8.
9.
10.

THINGS I WANT TO HAVE IN MY NEW HOME

WISHES

1.
2.
3.
4.
5.
6.
7.
8.

9.

10.

Before you start looking for a home, you should consider the following:

How much time do you want to spend commuting? Commuting is a big thing for many families. Traveling to and from work can sometimes be more stressful than the job itself. One thing you need to consider is how much time you want to spend traveling to and from work. Are there any highways or parkways close to the location you want to buy? Having easy access to the parkway or highway can make traveling a lot easier and a lot less stressful because you don't have to drive an extra 20 or 30 minutes to get where you want to go.

How close are the **local stores**? You may want to also looking into how far you are from the local supermarket, convenience stores, the library or even parks. If you buy a home in the boonies you may end up having to drive 20 minutes just to get a container of milk.

What **characteristics** of a home are important to you? Are you looking for a home with high ceilings or low ceilings? Do you want a home that has more modernized characteristics or do you want Victorian home? Do you want a basement or an attic? How big do you want the kitchen to be? Do you want a home with a lot of cabinet and closet space? Do you want a lot of property space? Is a big backyard important to you? Do you want a 1 or 2 car garage? These are just a few things to consider.

What minimum number of **bedrooms and bathrooms** do you want? If you are looking to expand and have kids in the future, you make want to give some serious consideration on how many bedrooms you are going to need. If you plan on entertaining guests, you may want to consider an extra room to use as a guestroom or maybe an extra room to use as a playroom. The worst thing to do is purchase a home without enough of living space. You don't want to feel cramp and an extension can be very costly. Why spend the money if you don't have too. The number of bathrooms is important too. Have only one full bath with a couple people in the home can be tough especially if the bathroom is being occupied or if you all get ready around the same time in the morning. You may want to look into 1 full bath and maybe one half bath as an option and if you can get a half bath in the master bedroom even better!

Are you looking for a specific school district? If you have kids or if you are planning to have kids then I cannot even stress the importance of purchasing a home in a location that ranks high in the quality of education they provide. Unfortunately, certain areas provide a better quality of education than others do. Some school districts provide more classes for children with learning disabilities and some offer more career oriented classes in high school such as culinary arts, hairdressing mechanics. These are things you want to take into consideration. If you go on the Internet you can find out what locations in your state provides excellent education for children based on test scores and curriculum. Education is the foundation for your child's future.

Are you willing to compromise the size or condition of the property to get that neighborhood? Many people are willing to sacrifice the size of the home for a better area because if you are not happy with the neighborhood then you are not going to be happy with the home you are purchasing. Additions can always be added in the future, but the people you live around, the amount of children in your area, your family's safety and better school districts cannot be added on.

What if you moved 20 minutes further from work, but had the extra bedroom for kids and more yard space for them to play or What if you commuted 10 minutes more, but had the extra garage space you always wanted to have in your new home? Would you be willing to make those sacrifices? Sometimes we need to give up certain things in order to get our perfect dream home. You need to consider what you are willing to sacrifice in order to receive your ideal home.

5. THE HOME MUST QUALIFY FOR A VA LOAN

VA Home Requirements

IF YOU DREAM IT, YOU CAN DO IT!

BUYING A HOME WITH A VA LOAN

A Dream Is Just a Dream
A Goal
Is a Dream with a Plan to Accomplish and Achieve That Dream

The Realty World
Helping Someone's Dream Become
"A Dream Come True"

The VA guarantees only the loan, NOT the condition of the property. It is the buyer's responsibility to be an educated buyer and make sure that what you are buying is satisfactory. This is where a realtor can help. A realtor will make sure that you buy a home that is suitable to all your needs.

What Are Main Home Requirements In Order To Be Approved For A VA Loan?

- ✓ The home must qualify
- ✓ At the present time the home must be **"livable"** Not livable in the future
- ✓ 600sf min.
- ✓ The house must have a stove and a sink with cabinets in kitchen
- ✓ Roof can't leak
- ✓ Heating must work
- ✓ No peeling paint
- ✓ No big holes in walls
- ✓ At least one working bath
- ✓ No **"stripped"** bathrooms or kitchen
- ✓ Garage door opener must have auto-reverse mechanism
- ✓ Must have minimum safety standards – smoke detectors, CO2 detectors

These minimum requirements rule out a large number of properties that veterans usually are attracted too! If you are hard working and physically fit, it may seem unfair that you must buy a home already fixed up, but that's the way the cookie crumbles!

6. THE ELIMINATION GAME

Learn How to Pick the Perfect Home for Your Family

IF YOU DREAM IT, YOU CAN DO IT!

BUYING A HOME WITH A VA LOAN

A Dream Is Just a Dream
A Goal
Is a Dream with a Plan to Accomplish and Achieve That Dream

The Elimination Game

The Realty World
Helping Someone's Dream Become
"A Dream Come True"

Your time has finally come to take the journey to homeownership. Let the fun begin! If you enjoy shopping and you, think buying a car is exciting then buying a home should feel like one of the best times in your life! Unfortunately, this is not always the case, but we can change that for you by playing, *"The Elimination Game."*

This game will help you narrow out your search so you can find your dream home. By using the right strategies and

techniques finding the home you want at a price that works within your budget can be a quick, easy, pleasant and memorable experience.

As we begin the *"The Elimination Game"* you will be astonished to discover how well you prioritized and prepared for buying a home. You will be faced with trade-offs, but ultimately it will help you buy the home you always dreamed of buying!

Step One:

First, we will create a search through the Multiple Listing Service using a program called Client Gateway. This enables a realtor to give you a direct look inside the MLS through the lens of your search criteria. Client Gateway is a software program in conjunction with the MLS, which will have a personal website for you and your realtor (me) to see all of the homes in all of the zip codes that match your criteria. You can even search for more than one home at a time on the same website, so if you can't decide whether you want a home with a 10 minute commute or a bigger home with a 30 minute commute. Our Multiple Listing Service at Client Gateway has the capabilities to look at both areas at the same time!

You can also leave comments on **Client Gateway** for each home and sort homes into **"favorites"**, **"possibilities"**, and **"rejects".**

HELPFUL TIP: The best thing about working with a real estate agent like me is that a real estate agent will know the area and the local market best. A real estate agent can also let you know if you have realistic expectations before you waste your time looking for a home that just does not exist or a home you are not going to be able to afford.

Round One of *"The Elimination Game"*

*If you have a few homes with vastly different criteria, then it is imperative that you take some time to use our **"The Elimination Game"** as a tool to help you narrow down your search to help you find the best home that will satisfy all your **wants** and **needs**.*

Step 1: Take 5-6 homes that you like from each zip code or neighborhood and drive around to see them. Maybe you need to drive straight from work to check commuting time or call/visit the local school.

Step 2: You and I may need to go look inside 3-4 homes to help you with your criteria

Step 3: By the end of the **first round**, you may still have two different neighborhoods with different trade-offs but not more than two

Round Two of *"The Elimination Game"*

Now it's time to really get to know where you want to live! You may have been able to skip the First Round because your search criteria were already well defined. We will schedule time to go look at these homes. You will see notes from me on your website letting you know pluses or minuses I see for any given home.

Together, we will look at each home for the following:

- ✓ Relative location
- ✓ What type of condition the home is in
- ✓ How well it meets your wants, needs and must-haves (Criteria)

Pitfalls & Expectations – the MLS listings will have **"creative photography"** remember that only the best views will be shown!

By the **END of the second round**, we may have found the right home but maybe not. We will have clarified your priorities and worked through your trade-offs (particularly if you are buying a home with your spouse). We may need to fine-tune your search now so you can see homes that specifically meet your criteria.

Round Three of *"The Elimination Game"*

Round three consists of…

Strategies and Techniques to Help You Narrow Your Search and Find Your Dream Home

- ✓ We may look at past comparable homes and realize that what you want does not fit the criteria (i.e. a single-family home in a multi-million dollar neighborhood for under $400k!)

- ✓ We keep a close eye on any new home shows up on the MLS that may be of interest to you!

- ✓ You will feel confident of home prices that match your criteria, so if a home pops up that is too high or too low, we will look at the reason for the pricing when we check it out.

Common Things to Consider

How will you know if it's the right home to make an offer? It should meet the majority of your criteria and the home you are interested in must be eligible for VA financing.

Unlike buying an investment, it has to "purchasing the home has to feel right" too. How will you know if it feels right? It becomes the home you compare all others.

Now you are ready for the next step: THE OFFER

THE OFFER

Real estate contracts in most states are and have always been pro-buyer, but were you aware that California has one of the most **"pro-buyer"** purchase agreements in the country! Buyers usually have a contingency period, in which they can complete home inspections, get their loan approved and accomplish any other things that are important before contingencies must be removed and they risk losing their initial deposit. What most people don't know is that a buyer needs to have a legitimate reason to cancel the contract, even during the contingency period.

The California Residential Purchase Contract (RPA) gives the buyer several "outs" that allow the buyer to cancel the contract without being penalized and losing the initial deposit. The "pro-buyer" purchase agreement is currently eight pages plus many disclosures.

Here at our realty office we will do the following:

- ✓ **The Review:** We will go over the purchase agreement page by page to make sure all of your questions are answered.

- ✓ **Price Lock:** Your offer will be structured to lock in a price and maximum interest rate while allowing you time to fully investigate any issues regarding the location of condition of the home.

- ✓ **Time Frame:** The offer will take as much as 90 minutes to fill out or as short as 15 min. (if you are already familiar with it).

- ✓ **Pre-approval:** Now your preparation begins to pay off! You have pre-approval from a lender and after all your hard work and dedication; you will have found the dream home you always wanted.

The Negotiations

Real Estate is one of the few places in America where some form of negotiation is the rule rather than the exception. Unfortunately, just because it is standard to negotiate when purchasing a home it doesn't mean that the majority of people in our society are actually good at it. Sure, most folks think that they are the "king of negotiators," but in reality, it is a learned skill that must be acquired through years of experience. It takes a clear understanding of the negotiation process in order to be good at it. This is why you need a realtor like me.

The Steps to a Successful Negotiation

- ✓ **Prepare:** Do your research ahead of time to so that you know your opponent and you know what you want from the negotiation.

- ✓ **Condition:** Consider buying the home in its "As Is" condition. This greatly reduces the risks of further price concessions from the seller. In many cases, it will allow you to purchase the home well below market value.

- ✓ **Offer Price:** Let the other side know what you want and let them tell you what they want.

- ✓ **Terms:** trade-off between price and time. First time buyers can usually move faster than repeat buyers, so quick closings can sometimes buy you a little lower purchase price or asking seller to pay for your closing costs.

- ✓ **Dispute:** Back-up your case with evidence and uncover defects in their argument.

- ✓ **Investigate:** Search for common ground and agreeable outcomes.

- ✓ **Hint:** Show that you are ready to reach an agreement.

- ✓ **Package:** Put together different agreeable options for both parties.

- ✓ **Close:** Come to an agreement and finalize the negotiation.

- ✓ **Keep Up On Things:** Ensure that their side, and yours, follows through with the negotiated agreement.

- ✓ **Competition:** Depends on the amount of competition, averaged market time for properties under $417k (conventional loan limit) is less than 60 days – still a "hot" market.

Escrow and the Investigations

After the buyer and seller of a home have established the terms and conditions for the transfer of ownership of that home (i.e. an accepted offer to purchase). An escrow will be opened with the agreed upon Escrow Provider. During the timelines specified in the purchase contract, all investigations by the buyer will be completed and all contractual obligations met, **such as:**

- ✓ **The Home inspection** - Your real estate agent has a list of inspectors from which you can choose to make sure the home you are purchasing is structurally sound, electrical and plumbing is up to code and works as it should, radon levels are at acceptable levels, and the home is free from wood-destroying insects. Your agent should be present for the inspections and will get a written report from the inspectors.

- ✓ **The Appraisal** - Your loan officer will order the VA appraisal. He/she will submit the appraisal request through the online portal of the Department of Veterans Affairs. The VA then randomly assigns an appraiser to your property. If the appraisal is less than the desired value and there is logical evidence to support it, an appraisal can be appealed.

- ✓ **A Request for Repairs (if needed)** - Repairs may be required for various reasons. For example, if the home does not pass the VA habitability inspection. Termite repairs may be required if the property did not receive a termite clearance. A request for repairs is tendered (purchases only). A seller is only required to provide termite clearance and to satisfy habitability issues.

- ✓ **Additional inspections or investigating the area can be done (i.e. schools, child care)**

The Countdown to Homeownership

The Review

Remember, **"Backwards planning"** in the military? On the other hand, maybe you were able to follow an SOP

(Standard Operating Procedure) and checklist for everything your job required. Here is your checklist with tasks to count down the days until the home is yours!

- 22. Make a Budget
- 21. Choose A Lending Institution and Apply For A VA Loan
- 20. Choose a Real Estate Agent
- 19. Start Looking For A Home!
- 18. Make An Offer!

1-2 Months before Closing

- 17. Sign the Finalized Purchase Agreement
- 16. Submit a Formal Loan Application
- 15. Choose a Real-Estate Attorney
- 13. Have the Home Inspected

- 12. Get Any Additions Inspections Done On the Home If Necessary
- 11. Review Pictures and Discoveries from Home Inspection
- 10. Review Rest of Disclosures from Seller/ Listing Agent

3-5 Weeks Before Closing

- 9. Get Homeowners' Insurance

2-4 Weeks before Closing

- 8. Arrange For Utilities at New Home
- 7. Receive Official VA Loan Letter from Lender

1 Week before Closing

- 6. Receive Copy of Settlement Statement
- 5. Final Walk Through Of the House
- 4. A Small Victory Dance for Getting To This Milestone

- 3. Do Any Last Minute Preparation For Packing!
- 2. Meet Me At 5pm To Get The Keys!
- 1. **Congratulations!** You Now Have A Piece Of The American Dream!

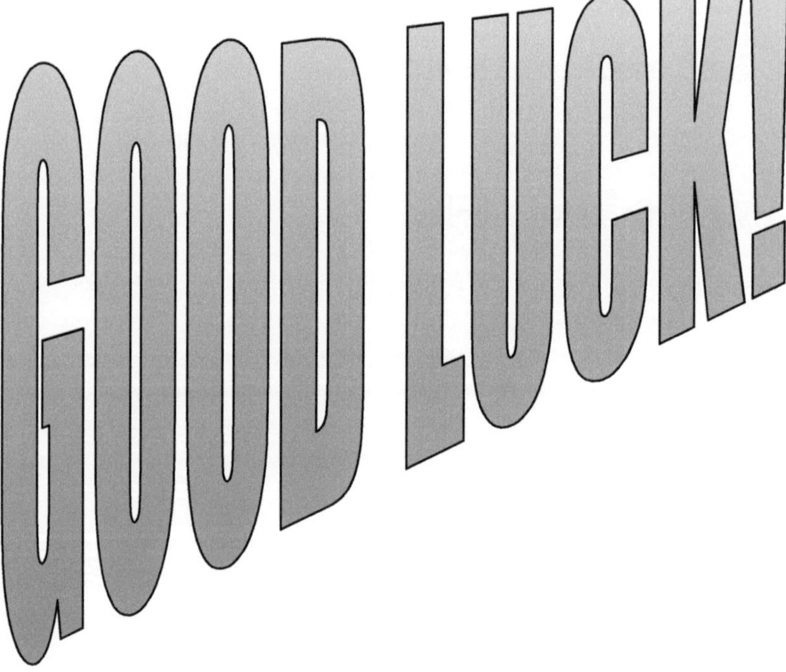

Author Stacey Chillemi

New Jersey-based freelance writer, providing worldwide professional freelance writing services.

Summary: Stacey Chillemi graduated from Richard Stockton College in Pomona, New Jersey, majoring in marketing and advertisement. In the mid-nineties while in college, she began her first book, Epilepsy: You're Not Alone. It was published six years later. Before and after graduation in 1996, she worked in New York City for NBC. Since the birth of her children, she has been a freelance journalist.

She has written features for journals and newspapers. Her articles have appeared in dozens of newspapers and magazines in North America and abroad. She won an award from the Epilepsy

Foundation of America in 2002 for her help and dedication to people with epilepsy.

Accomplishments:

- Writer for Neurology Now Magazine (The Academic Academy of Neurology – The Epilepsy Column) February 2010
- February 2010, Wrote an article about Epilepsy & Menstruation with Dr. Devinsky (Epileptologist from NYU)
- Book Signing at Borders in Freehold, New Jersey for Faith, Courage, Wisdom, Strength and Hope" - July 2009
- H.O.P.E. Mentor, for the Epilepsy Foundation
- Speaker at different events for schools, organizations, political events
- Spoke in front of Congress in Washington for employment discrimination for people with Epilepsy
- Appeared on four talk shows to discuss epilepsy focusing on the importance of understanding epilepsy, how to help someone having a seizure and giving people with epilepsy encouragement and hope for the future.
- Appeared on radio stations discussing epilepsy
- Appeared on the Michael Dressor Show - Health Radio

- Appeared in newspapers all over New Jersey such as, The Leader, Belleville Post and the Star Ledger.
- Received awards in my achievements and certificates in recognition for outstanding efforts in trying to improve society.
- Active participant in organizations and activities.
- Published over 400 articles
- Author has a dynamic personality and strong public speaking skills.

BOOKS PUBLISHED BY STACEY CHILLEMI:

- The Complete Herbal Guide: A Natural Approach to Healing the Body
- How to Live Comfortably with Asthma
- Epilepsy You're Not Alone
- Eternal Love: Romantic Poetry Straight from the Heart
- My Mommy Has Epilepsy (Children's Book)
- My Daddy Has Epilepsy (Children's Book)
- Keep the Faith: To Live and Be Heard from the Heavens Above (poetry book)
- Live, Learn, and Be Happy with Epilepsy
- Epilepsy and Pregnancy: What Every Woman Should Know Co-authored by Dr. Blanca Vasques
- Faith, Courage, Wisdom, Strength and Hope

- How to Be Wealthy Selling Informational Products on the Internet
- How to Become Wealthy in Real Estate
- How to Become Wealthy Selling Ebooks
- Life's Missing Instruction Manual: Beyond Words
- How To Become Wealthy Selling Products on The Internet
- Breast Cancer: Questions, Answers & Self-Help Techniques
- How Thinking Positive Can Make You Successful: Master The Power Of Positive Thinking

STACEY CHILLEMI STORIES AND POETRY HAVE BEEN PUBLISHED IN:

- Chicken Soup for the Recovering Soul
- Chicken Soup for the Shoppers Soul
- Whispers of Inspiration

NBC Network
New York City

- Worked for NBC on Dateline
- Worked for Channel 4 News
- Worked for the Today Show

The Journal Magazine

Journalist

Wrote comments on topics of reader interest to stimulate and mold public opinion, in accordance with viewpoints and policies of publication.

Editor of UZURI Fashion Magazine

Awards: June 26, 2002, I was honored an award by the Epilepsy Foundation of New Jersey for Outstanding Volunteer Award.

Web sites: http://www.authorsden.com/staceydchillemi

http://www.lulu.com/spotlight/staceychil

http://freelanceinternational.viviti.com

Bibliography

Center, V. M. (2011). Get your VA and FHA Checklist in order. *VA Loan Library* , 1.

Estate, D. R. (2011). FIVE POWER CONTRACT NEGOTIATING TIPS . 1.

Frequently Asked Questions. (2011). *VALOANS* , 1.

Goverment Va Loans. (2011). *home loans* , p. 12.

Housing, O. o. (2011). The Home Buying Guide. *U.S. Department of Housing and Urban Development* , 8.

Lamar, R. (2011). Backing out of a Real Estate Contract: Buyer's Rights. *Racheal Real Estate Blog* , 1.

Loan Guide. (2011). *Direct VA Loans* .

site, G. (2011). VA Loan Qualifications. *Department of Veteran Affairs* .

STREITFELD, D. (2011). Federal Retreat on Bigger Loans Rattles Housing. *New York Tomes* , 1.

ISBN: 978-1-105-52392-2